KETO DESSERTS COOKBOOK #2020

Best Keto-Friendly Treats for Your Low-Carb Sweet Tooth, Fat Burning & Disease Reversal.

Francis Michael

ISBN: 978-1-952504-24-2
COPYRIGHT © 2020 by Francis Michael

All rights reserved. This book is copyright protected and it's for personal use only. Without the prior written permission of the publisher, no part of this publication should be reproduced, distributed, or transmitted in any form or by any means, including photocopying, recording, or other electronic or mechanical methods. This publication is sold with the idea that the publisher is not required to render accounting, officially permitted, or otherwise, qualified services. Seek for the services of a legal or professional, a practiced individual in the profession if advice is needed.

DISCLAIMER

The information contained in this book is geared for educational and entertainment purposes only. Strenuous efforts have been made towards providing accurate, up to date and reliable complete information. The information in this book is true and complete to the best of our knowledge. Neither the publisher nor the author takes any responsibility for any possible consequences of reading or enjoying the recipes in this book. The author and publisher disclaim any liability in connection with the use of information contained in this book. Under no circumstance will any legal responsibility or blame be apportioned against the author or publisher for any reparation, damages, or monetary loss due to the information herein, either directly or indirectly.

Table of Contents

INTRODUCTION 7

Keto Desserts Must-Have Ingredients 7

CAKES 8

Pound Cake 8

Blueberry Cheesecake Bites 9

Carrot Cake 11

Rainbow Cake 13

Chantilly Cake 15

Lava Cake 17

Chocolates Zucchini Cake 18

Lemon Cupcakes 20

Vanilla Berry Mug Cake 22

Jaffa Cheesecake 23

Cinnamon Tea Cake 24

Birthday Cake 25

Butter Cake 27

Strawberry Cream Cake 29

COOKIES 31

Soft n' Chewy Cookies 31

Sugar Cookie Macaroons 32

Chocolate Almond Biscotti 33

Fudge Cookies 35

Candied Bourbon Pecans 36
Pecan Snowball Cookies 37
Chocolate Chip 38
Flourless Chocolate Cookies 39
Almond Flour 40
Peanut Butter Bacon Cookies 41
Bacon Onion Cookies 42
Butter Cookie Energy Bites 44
Snickerdoodle Cookies 45
Chewy Pecan Cookies 47
Pumpkin Cream Cheese 48

BARS 49

Peanut Butter Chocolate Bars 49
S'mores Bars 50
Chocolate Fudge Protein Bars 52
Cookie Bars 53
Twix Bars 54
Magic Bars 56
Crunch Bars 57

TARTS 58

Keto Tarts 58
Lemon Curd Tarts 60
Cheesecake Tarts 61

- Chocolate Tart 63
- Tart Dough 64
- Peanut Butter Tarts 65
- Hazelnut Tart 67
- Tart Crust 68
- Caramel Tarts 69

PIES 71

- Strawberry Pie 71
- Butter Pie 72
- Spinach Pie 73
- Coconut Custard Pie 74
- Almond Butter Pie 75
- Almond Flour Pie Crust 76
- Chocolate Pie Crust 77

FROZEN DESSERTS 78

- Vanilla Ice Cream 78
- Butter Pecan Ice Cream 79
- Chocolate Mason Jar Ice Cream 80
- Strawberry Ice Cream 81
- Lime Popsicles 82
- Raspberry Ripple Ice Cream 83
- Shamrock Shake 84
- Ice Cream Sandwiches 85

CUSTARDS & MOUSSES 87
- Vanilla Cheesecake Mousse 87
- Chocolate Custard 88
- Coconut Mousse 89
- Crème Anglaise Custard 90
- Peanut Butter Mousse 91
- Pumpkin Cheesecake Mousse 92
- Egg Custard 93
- Mascarpone Mousse 94

INTRODUCTION

Keto Desserts Must-Have Ingredients

1. **Full-Fat Dairy Products:**

Dairy products like heavy cream, cream cheese, sour cream, and butter are good ketogenic diet ingredients to have on hand.

2. **Almond Flour:**

Substitute the wheat flour with almond flour. It's higher in fat, protein, and fiber, but also much higher in nutrient value. You can buy almond flour in supermarkets.

3. **Coconut Flour:**

Coconut flour can serve as an alternative for gluten free and nut free flour. It lasts a longer period of time because the ratios for coconut flour to wheat flour are quite different. You can order your coconut flour online.

4. **Coconut Oil:**

Coconut oil has lots of uses and its always advisable to have two on hand at all times. It can be used for cooking and in daily beauty routine.

5. **Coconut Milk:**

Coconut milk can be substituted for milk. Milk can be used in baked goods but it is usually high in carbs. Coconut milk can be used as a high fat, low carb substitute for milk.

6. **Sugar Substitutes:**

There is need to substitute refined sugars in your keto desserts because sugars are usually high in carbs. It is important to have a substitute on hand for your sweet keto treats.

7. **Almond Butter:**

Almond butter is a good substitute or keto desserts. Many recipes call for peanut butter, but I prefer almond.

8. **Sugar-Free Dark Chocolate:**

It is good to use sugar-free dark chocolate when you crave for chocolate. There are lots of chocolate treats that utilize sugar-free dark chocolate.

CAKES

Pound Cake

Preparation time: 10 minutes

Cooking time: 40 minutes

Total time 50 minutes

Serves: 6 to 8 people

Recipe Ingredients:

- 5 large eggs
- 115 g full-fat cream cheese, 4 ounces
- ¼ cup of melted butter or ghee (60 ml/2 fl. oz)
- ¼ cup of heavy cream (60 ml/2 fl. oz)
- 2 teaspoons of sugar-free vanilla extract
- 1 teaspoon of sugar-free almond extract
- 1½ cups of almond flour (150g/5.3 oz)
- ½ cup of granulated Swerve or Erythritol, or to taste (100g/3.5 oz)
- Pinch of sea salt

Cooking Instructions:

1. Start by heating your oven to 350°F (conventional), or 310°F (fan assisted).

2. Then line a loaf pan with parchment paper. In a large mixing bowl, add the eggs, cream cheese, butter, cream, vanilla, and almond extract.

3. Beat them together using a hand mixer until smooth. Add in the remaining dry ingredients and beat once more.

4. Transfer the batter to the prepared loaf pan. Bake for about 30 to 40 minutes until a toothpick inserted into the middle comes out clean.

5. The wider the loaf pan, the less time it will take to cook through. Optionally, dust with some powdered Swerve or Erythritol.

6. Serve with some whipped cream and enjoy!

Blueberry Cheesecake Bites

Preparation time: 20 minutes

Cooking time: 40 minutes

Overall time: 1 hour

Serves: 6 to 8 people

Recipe Ingredients:

Lemon Cookie Crust

- 2 packs of fat snax lemony lemon
- 2 tablespoons of front porch pecans unsalted
- 1 tablespoon of salted butter melted
- 1 tablespoon of keto brown sugar replacement

Lemon Cheesecake

- 8 ounces cream cheese softened
- ¼ cup of sour cream
- 1 tablespoon of lemon juice
- ¼ cup of granular monk fruit Erythritol granular or swerve, granular
- 1 large egg
- ½ teaspoon of vanilla extract
- ¼ teaspoon of lemon zest

Blueberry Topping

- 1 cup of Blueberries
- We used frozen
- 2 tablespoon of granular monk fruit Erythritol granular or swerve, granular
- 1 tablespoon of lemon juice
- 1 scoop of collagen peptides (Unflavored)

Cooking Instructions:

1. Start by heating the oven to 350°F. In a food processor, make the crust by mixing all of the ingredients.

2. Then line the muffin tins with mini or standard silicone molds. Divide the crust across the muffin tins.

3. Press it down to form a solid base. Then bake for about 3 minutes (if using a mini•muffin pan), or 5 minutes (if using a standard muffin pan).

4. After baking, set them aside. Turn the oven to 300°F, add in all cheesecake ingredients to a stand mixer and blend until smooth.

5. Divide the cheesecake mixture among the muffin tins. Add water to the bottom of a baking sheet • this is the water bath for the cheesecake.

6. Add the muffin tin to the baking sheet, serve and enjoy!

Carrot Cake

Preparation time: 30 minutes

Cooking time: 30 minutes

Total time: 1 hour

Serves: 20 people:

Recipe Ingredients

Dry Ingredients

- 1½ cups of almond flour
- ¼ cup of coconut flour
- 1 tablespoon of baking powder
- 1 teaspoon of ground cinnamon
- 2 scoops collagen peptides, Unflavored

Wet Ingredients

- 1 cup of butter melted
- ¼ cup of MCT oil
- 4 large eggs
- 1¼ cup powdered monk fruit Erythritol

Filling Ingredients

- 2 cups of shredded carrots
- 1 cup of shredded unsweetened coconut
- ¼ cup of raisins no sugar added
- 1 cup of pecans, chopped
- 2 teaspoons of vanilla extract
- 1 cup of crushed pineapples (in juice) no sugar added

Frosting Ingredients

- 1 cup of butter melted
- 1.5 cups of powdered monk fruit Erythritol
- 2 teaspoons of vanilla extract
- 16 ounces of cream cheese, softened

Cooking Instructions:

1. Start by heating your oven to 350°F. Then, whisk the dry ingredients together in a small bowl. Set aside.

2. In a large mixing bowl, whisk the wet ingredients together, set aside. Mix the filling ingredients. Set aside.

3. Add in the dry ingredients to the wet ingredients. Fold in with a spatula. Fold in the filling ingredients. Divide the batter into 9in cake pans.

4. Slam the cake pans to level the batter. Bake for about 30 to 40 minutes, until a toothpick comes out clean.

5. When the time is up, allow to cool for about 30 minutes before frosting. Mix all of the frosting ingredients in a stand-mixer (3 minutes).

6. Frost and design the cakes as you desire. Serve and enjoy!

Rainbow Cake

Preparation time: 20 minutes

Cooking time: 25 minutes

Overall time: 45 minutes

Yield: 8 slices

Recipe Ingredients:

Cake:

- ½ cup of coconut flour
- 2 cups of almond flour
- 4 tablespoons of butter
- 1 cup of Erythritol
- ¼ cup of olive oil
- 2 teaspoons of vanilla extract
- 2 teaspoons of baking powder
- 6 large of eggs
- 1 teaspoon of baking soda
- 1 teaspoon of pink salt
- 4 tablespoons of heavy cream

Frosting:

- 1 cup of Erythritol, powdered
- 6-ounces cream cheese
- ½ cup of heavy cream
- 10 drops of liquid stevia
- 2 teaspoons of vanilla extract

Cooking Instructions:

1. Start by heating the oven to 350°F. Add the butter to a microwave safe bowl and melt. Then add in the remaining wet ingredients into the bowl with butter.

2. Add all the dry ingredients in a separate mixing bowl, and mix well. Mix all of the ingredients together.

3. If making the cake rainbow split up evenly into 6 separate bowls and add in the food coloring into the mixes.

4. Place them in the cake pans and place in the oven for 25 minutes. For the frosting, ensure that the cream cheese is at room temperature.

5. Place the heavy cream into a mixing bowl, use a hand mixer to mix them together until fluffy. Add in the remaining ingredients and mix well.

6. Once cakes are cool add a layer of frosting to each layer then stack. Frost the rest of the cake. Serve and enjoy!

Chantilly Cake

Preparation time: 10 minutes

Cooking time: 45 minutes

Total time: 55 minutes

Serves: 6 to 8 people

Recipe Ingredients:

Cake:

- 2 cups of (8oz) almond flour
- ½ cup of (2oz) coconut flour
- ½ cup of (3.5oz) Erythritol
- 2 teaspoons baking powder
- 1 teaspoon of baking soda
- ½ teaspoon pink salt
- 6 large eggs
- 1 teaspoon of vanilla extract
- 6 ounces of butter
- 20 drops of liquid stevia
- ¼ cup of heavy cream
- 1 tablespoon of almond extract

Frosting:

- 16 ounces of cream cheese
- ¾ cup of heavy cream
- 1 tablespoon of almond extract
- ¼ cup of Erythritol, powdered

Topping:

- ½ cup of blueberries
- ½ cup of raspberries
- ½ cup of strawberries
- ½ cup of blackberries

Cooking Instructions:

1. Start by heating your oven to 350°F.

2. In a medium mixing bowl, add in all the dry cake ingredients almond flour, coconut flour, erythritol, baking powder, baking soda, and salt. Mix them together until well combined.

3. Melt butter and add all of the wet cake ingredients butter, eggs, vanilla extract, stevia, heavy cream, and almond extract together in a separate mixing bowl.

4. Add in the dry ingredients into the wet ingredients and give everything a good stir to combine.

5. Pour it all in one pan and cut it in halt if you want a middle filling. Bake for about 45 minutes until the tooth pick comes out clean. The top may get a little brown.

6. For the frosting, set your cream cheese out to get to room temperature. Add all of the frosting ingredients including the cream cheese together.

7. Use a hand mixer to mix them together. Let the cakes cool for about 15 to 20 minutes.

8. Then frost, add the berries to the middle and the top. Serve and enjoy!

Lava Cake

Preparation time: 5 minutes

Cooking time: 10 minutes

Overall time: 15 minutes

Serves: 2 people

Recipe Ingredients:

- 4 tablespoons of cocoa powder
- 2 tablespoons of powdered swerve
- ½ teaspoon baking powder
- 1/8 teaspoon of kosher salt
- 2 medium eggs
- 2 tablespoons of heavy whipping cream
- 2 teaspoons of pure vanilla extract

Cooking Instructions:

1. Start by heating your oven to 350°F. Prepare 8 ounces ramekins or other small glass baking dishes with cooking spray.

2. In a medium mixing bowl, mix all dry ingredients together with a fork to remove lumps. Beat the eggs in a separate mixing bowl.

3. Add heavy cream and vanilla, whisk them together to combine. Then combine the wet and dry ingredients together.

4. Stir until well combined and smooth. Divide the batter between the two prepared dishes. Bake in oven on middle rack for about 10 to 15 minutes.

5. When the time is up, remove and serve.

Chocolates Zucchini Cake

Preparation time: 10 minutes

Cooking time: 30 minutes

Total time: 40 minutes

Yield: 12 slices

Recipe Ingredients:

Chocolate Zucchini Cake:

- 4 medium eggs
- ½ butter, melted
- 4 tablespoons of almond milk
- 1 cup of shredded zucchini
- 2/3 cup of almond flour
- 1/3 cup of coconut flour
- ½ cup of cocoa powder
- ½ cup stevia or any sweetener of your choice
- 1 teaspoon of baking powder

Chocolate Ganache:

- 200g of dark chocolate
- 3 tablespoons of butter
- 4 tablespoons of milk

Cooking Instructions:

Chocolate Zucchini Cake:

1. Mix the coconut flour, cocoa powder, stevia, and baking powder in a large mixing bowl.

2. Add the eggs, almond milk and melted butter. Mix them together to combine. Spread out into greased pan.

3. Bake at 360°F for about 30 to 40 minutes or until a toothpick inserted comes out clean.

Chocolate Ganache:

1. Microwave all ingredients for about 2 minutes, opening the door, once in a while, to stir.

4. Once the cake is cool, frost with chocolate ganache if you desire.

5. Serve and enjoy!

Lemon Cupcakes

Preparation time: 10 minutes

Cooking time: 12 minutes

Overall time: 22 minutes

Serves: 48 people

Recipe Ingredients:

Low carb lemon cupcakes:

- 2 whole/120g/4 ounces of sweet lemons quartered, we used Meyer lemons.
- 6 medium eggs
- 250g of almond meal/flour
- 1 teaspoon of baking powder
- 4 tablespoons of granulated sweetener of choice or more if necessary
- 1 teaspoon of vanilla
- ¼ teaspoon of salt

Lemon icing/frosting:

- 125 ml natural yoghurt unsweetened
- 110g cream cheese softened
- Granulated sweetener of choice to taste
- Lemon zest and juice to taste

Cooking Instructions:

Low Carb Lemon Cupcakes:

1. In your food processor, place the lemon quarters and ensure to remove any seeds.

2. Using the blade attachment, blitz until almost pureed. Then add in all the other ingredients. Pulse until smooth.

3. Place a spoon of the batter into each mini cupcake case and bake at 350°F for about 10 to 12 minutes until a toothpick comes out clean.

Lemon Icing/Frosting:

1. Mix the softened cream cheese with the natural yoghurt with a fork until smooth.

4. Add the lemon zest and juice. Add in stevia or sweeter to your taste. When the cupcakes are completely cold.

5. Decorate the low carb lemon cupcakes with the icing/frosting. Top each one with a tiny piece of lemon.

6. Serve and enjoy!

Vanilla Berry Mug Cake

Preparation time: 5 minutes

Cooking time: 1 minute

Total Time: 6 minutes

Serves: 1

Recipe Ingredients:

- 1 tablespoon of butter, melted
- 2 tablespoons of cream cheese full fat
- 2 tablespoons of coconut flour
- 1 tablespoon of granulated sweetener of choice or more to taste
- 1 teaspoon of vanilla extract
- ¼ teaspoon of baking powder
- 1 medium egg
- 6 frozen raspberries

Cooking Instructions:

1. Place the butter and cream cheese in your chosen mug. Microwave on High for about 20 seconds.

2. Add the coconut flour, sweetener, vanilla, and baking powder. Mix them together. Add in egg, and mix again.

3. Scrape down the sides of the mug, then press in 6 frozen raspberries into the cake batter.

4. Microwave on High for about 1 minute 20 seconds. When the time is up.

5. Serve and enjoy!

Jaffa Cheesecake

Preparation time: 15 minutes

Total Time: 15 minutes

Serves: 10 people

Recipe Ingredients:

Jaffa Cheesecake base:

- 55g of butter, melted
- 150g of almond meal/flour
- 45g of cocoa unsweetened
- 2 tablespoons of granulated sweetener, of choice or more

Jaffa Cheesecake:

- 2 orange sugar free jelly 500ml/4 serve size
- 500ml boiling water
- 500g cream cheese full fat, not spreadable
- 90% chocolate optional to decorate

Cooking Instructions:

Jaffa Cheesecake Base:

1. Mix the melted butter, almond meal/flour, cocoa and sweetener together.
2. Press into a greased and lined dish. Press down firmly with the back of a spoon or the bottom of a glass. Place in the fridge to harden.

Jaffa Cheesecake:

1. Pour the two-orange sugar free jelly boxes/sachets into a pouring jug and add 500ml of boiling water. Give everything a good stir to dissolve.
2. Cut the cream cheese into chunks and add to the boiling jelly mixture. Using a stick blender with the blade attachment, puree until smooth and lump free.
3. Pour the jelly and cream cheese mixture onto the prepared cheesecake base and place back into the refrigerator to set for a few hours.
4. Melt some dark 90% chocolate and drizzle over the top of the Jaffa cheesecake. Serve and enjoy!

Cinnamon Tea Cake

Preparation time: 15 minutes

Cooking time: 20 minutes

Overall time: 35 minutes

Serves: 6 to 8 people

Recipe Ingredients:

- 3.5 oz. unsalted butter softened
- ¼ cup of swerve
- 2 medium eggs
- 1 tsp. of vanilla essence
- 1¼ cup of almond flour
- 1 tsp. of baking powder
- ¼ cup of unsweetened almond milk
- 2 tbsp. of unsalted butter melted, for topping
- 1 tbsp. of swerve for topping
- 1 tsp. of cinnamon for topping

Cooking Instructions:

1. Start by heating your oven to 340°F. Prepare an 8-inch round cake tin by greasing and lining the base with parchment paper.

2. In a medium bowl, Place the butter and swerve. Blend with your hand mixer on medium speed until smooth and creamy.

3. Add the eggs one at a time and beat them in. Add the rest ingredients, except the topping ingredients. Mix on low speed until well combined.

4. Gently spoon the mixture into your prepared tin. Bake for about 20 to 25 minutes, until the cake is lightly browned. When the time is up.

5. Allow to cool in the tin for about 10 minutes before turning out onto a cooling rack. In a medium bowl, mix the swerve and cinnamon together.

6. Brush the warm cake with the melted butter and sprinkle over the cinnamon mixture. Serve the cake warm.

Birthday Cake

Preparation time: 20 minutes

Cooking time: 1 hour

Overall time: 1 hr. 20 minutes

Serves: 24 people

Recipe Ingredients:

Cake:

- 1 cup of Erythritol
- ¾ cup of butter, softened
- 8 large egg
- ½ cup of unsweetened almond milk
- 1 tablespoon of vanilla extract
- 3 cups of blanched almond flour
- ½ cup of coconut flour
- 1½ tablespoon of gluten-free baking powder

Cream cheese frosting:

- 32 ounces cream cheese, softened
- 1/3 cup of butter, softened
- 2/3 cup of powdered erythritol
- 1 teaspoon of vanilla extract

Cooking Instructions:

Cake:

1. Heat your oven to 350°F. Line the bottom of a 9 in (23 cm) round springform pan with parchment paper.

2. Beat together the erythritol and butter in a large mixing bowl, until fluffy. Beat in the eggs, one at a time, then the almond milk and vanilla extract.

3. Beat in the almond flour, coconut flour, and gluten-free baking powder. Transfer 1/3 of the dough to the lined pan and smooth the top with a spatula.

4. Bake for about 18 to 22 minutes, until the top is lightly golden. Repeat with another 1/3 of the dough, then again with the final 1/3 (making 3 layers total).

Make the frosting:

1. Beat together the cream cheese, butter, powdered erythritol, and vanilla extract, until smooth.

2. Let the cake layers cool separately to room temp before stacking. Frost between the layers, and all over the top and sides at the end.

3. Top with chopped pecans if you desire.

4. Serve and enjoy!

Butter Cake

Preparation time: 10 minutes

Cooking time: 35 minutes

Overall time: 45 minutes

Recipe Ingredients:

- 3 tablespoons of coconut flour
- ¼ cup of powdered erythritol
- 1 teaspoon of baking powder
- 1 tablespoon of beef gelatin (optional)
- 8 tablespoons of butter, room temp.
- ½ teaspoon of vanilla extract
- 2 large eggs, room temp.

Top Layer:

- 8 tablespoons of butter, room temp.
- 8 ounces cream cheese, room temp.
- ¼ cup of powdered erythritol
- ½ teaspoon of vanilla extract
- 50 drops of liquid stevia
- 2 large eggs, room temp.

Cooking Instructions:

1. Heat your oven to 350°F. Grease an 8-inch spring form pan with coconut oil spray.

2. Bottom Layer: In a large mixing bowl, add the butter, vanilla extract and eggs combine using a hand mixer.

3. Add the coconut flour, erythritol, baking powder and optionally the gelatin, and combine using a spatula. Set aside.

4. Top Layer: In a large bowl, cream together the butter and cream cheese using a hand mixer.

5. Add in the vanilla extract, erythritol, stevia and eggs, mix them together to combine until smooth.

6. Cake form the bottom layer (effectively the cake's "crust") into the bottom of the spring form pan using your hands.

7. Pour the top layer on top of the crust layer and give it a few taps to release the air bubbles.

8. Bake for about 30 to 35 minutes or until the sides are browned. Allow to cool for about 15 to 20 minutes to let cake set before removing from pans.

9. Serve and enjoy!

Strawberry Cream Cake

Preparation time: 10 minutes

Cooking time: 20 minutes

Additional time: 1 hour

Overall time: 1 hr. 30 minutes

Yield: 12 slices

Recipe Ingredients:

For the cake:

- 6 tbsp. of butter, melted
- ⅓ cup of heavy cream
- 4 large eggs
- 2 tsp. of vanilla extract
- ½ cup of coconut flour
- ¼ cup of xylitol
- 1 tbsp. of stevia blend, optional
- ½ tsp. of salt
- ¼ tsp. of baking soda

For the whipped cream:

- 1 cup of whipping cream
- 1 tsp. of vanilla
- 1 tbsp. of powdered sweetener, optional

For the strawberries:

- 1 cup of sliced strawberries
- 2 tsp. of xylitol, if needed

Cooking Instructions:

1. Heat your oven to 350°F. Spray an 8x8 square baking dish with non-stick spray.

2. In a medium mixing bowl, add the melted butter, heavy cream, eggs, and vanilla. Mix with an electric mixer until well combined.

3. Then add the coconut flour, xylitol, stevia, salt, and baking soda to the bowl and give everything a good stir to combine.

4. Spread the batter into the prepared baking dish and place in the oven. Bake in your oven for about 15 to 20 minutes.

5. Bake until the top springs back when lightly touched and a toothpick comes out clean. When the time is up, allow to cool completely.

6. To make the whipped cream, beat together the cold whipping cream, vanilla, and sweetener until stiff peaks form.

7. Spread the whipped cream over the cake. Taste the strawberries and sprinkle with sweetener, if necessary.

8. Cut the cake into 9 slices and top with strawberries when serving. Serve and enjoy!

COOKIES

Soft n' Chewy Cookies

Preparation time: 10 minutes

Cooking time: 15 minutes

Overall time: 25 minutes

Serves: 6 to 8 people

Recipe Ingredients:

- ¾ cup of almond meal
- ¼ cup of shredded coconut
- 1 tbsp. of baking powder
- ½ tsp. of stevia
- 1 tbsp. of coconut oil, melted
- 1 tsp. of vanilla extract
- 2 large eggs

Cooking Instructions:

1. In a mixing bowl, combine the almond meal, shredded coconut, stevia, and baking powder.

2. In a separate bowl, combine the wet ingredients and then add them to the dry ingredients. Mix together until well combined.

3. Drop dough on a cookie sheet (preferably covered with a silicone baking mat) about 2" apart. Makes eight large cookies or twelve small cookies.

4. Bake in your oven at 375°F for about 15 minutes. When the time is up, allow the cookies to cool completely on a wire rack before eating.

5. Serve and enjoy!

Sugar Cookie Macaroons

Preparation time: 5 minutes

Cooking time: 15 minutes

Overall time: 20 minutes

Serves: 10 to 12 people

Recipe Ingredients:

- 2 tablespoons of butter, melted
- ¼ teaspoon of vanilla extract
- 8 drops od Capella buttercream concentrate (omit if you want standard macaroons)
- 1 large egg
- ¼ cup of swerve confectioners
- ½ cup of unsweetened macaroon coconut (or unsweetened shredded coconut)
- 2 tablespoons of coconut flour
- granular erythritol (to sprinkle on top; omit if you want standard macaroons)

Cooking Instructions:

1. Heat your oven to 375°F. Combine melted butter, vanilla extract, buttercream extract (omit for regular macaroons), and an egg in a medium mixing bowl.

2. Beat them together with a fork until well combined. In a mixing bowl, combine swerve confectioners, macaroon coconut (or coconut flakes), and coconut flour.

3. Mix everything together until well combined. Then add the wet ingredients to the dry ingredients and combine.

4. Onto a non-stick cookie sheet, scoop out tbsp. sized macaroons. Then, sprinkle a bit of granular erythritol on top of each unbaked macaroon (omit for regular macaroons).

5. Bake in your oven at 375°F for about 12 to 15 minutes, when the time is up. Allow to cool before serving.

6. Serve and enjoy!

Chocolate Almond Biscotti

Preparation time: 10 minutes

Cooking time: 45 minutes

Overall time: 55 minutes

Serves: 14 people

Recipe Ingredients:

- 1.5 cup of almond flour Bob's Red Mill
- ½ cup of unsweetened cocoa powder
- ½ cup of swerve confectioners' sweetener
- 2 tablespoons of protein powder unflavored (we used Jay Robbs)
- 1 teaspoon of baking powder
- 1 teaspoon of guar gum or xanthan
- ½ teaspoon of salt
- 8 tablespoons of butter, melted
- 1 teaspoon of almond extract
- ½ teaspoon of vanilla liquid stevia
- 2 eggs beaten
- ½ cup of almonds, sliced
- 6 oz. sugar free chocolate chips optional
- 2 oz. almonds toasted, chopped

Cooking Instructions:

1. Heat your oven to 325°F. Blend the first 7 dry ingredients in a stand mixer, blend on low to combine.

2. Add in the remaining ingredients, expect almonds and blend until well incorporated.

3. Stir in the almonds and place the dough on a baking pan lined with parchment. Form a rectangle about 10 inches in length and 6 inches width.

4. Bake in your oven for about 30 minutes. When the time is up, allow to cool for about 30 minutes before slicing.

5. Gently lay the biscotti flat on the pan, cut side down, to continue to bake another 15 minutes.

6. Remove from oven and allow to cool before handling. Gently flip biscotti over and bake for another 10 minutes more.

7. Allow to cool completely before adding optional toppings if you desire. If using optional toppings.

8. Dip one end of the biscotti in melted chocolate then add chopped toasted almonds. Place in refrigerator to set.

9. Serve and enjoy!

Fudge Cookies

Preparation time: 5 minutes

Cooking time: 2 hours

Overall time: 2 hr. 5 minutes

Recipe Ingredients:

- 2½ cups of sugar-free chocolate chips
- 1/3 cup of coconut milk
- 1 teaspoon of pure vanilla extract
- A dash of salt
- 2 tsp. of vanilla liquid stevia (optional)

Cooking Instructions:

1. Start by stirring coconut milk, chocolate chips, vanilla, stevia and salt in a small 3- or 4-quart crock pot.

2. Cover and cook on low for about 2 hours. Uncover, turn off and let sit for 30 minutes to 1 hour (Don't stir).

3. Stir well for 5 minutes until smooth. Line a one-quart casserole dish with parchment paper and spread mixture in.

4. Chill 30 minutes or until firm. Serve and enjoy!

Candied Bourbon Pecans

Preparation time: 5 minutes

Cooking time: 20 minutes

Total time: 25 minutes

Recipe Ingredients:

- ¼ cup of butter melted
- 1 tbsp. of sugar free maple syrup
- 2 tbsp. of bourbon optional
- 1 teaspoon of maple extract
- ½ cup of swerve sweetener or another sugar free sweetener
- 1 tsp. of ground cinnamon
- 2.5 cups of pecans raw, unsalted

Cooking Instructions:

1. Preheat your oven to 325°F. In a mixing bowl, whisk the butter and syrup until combined.

2. Add the bourbon (optional) and maple extract and stir until incorporated. Stir in the Swerve and cinnamon.

3. Place pecans in a bowl and toss together with coating. Spread them on a greased baking sheet.

4. Bake for about 15 minutes. Once out of the oven while the juices on the pan are still hot, use a spatula to toss the pecans.

5. Allow to cool before storing in an airtight container.

Pecan Snowball Cookies

Preparation time: 5 minutes

Cooking time: 15 minutes

Total time: 20 minutes

Serves: 2 people

Recipe Ingredients:

- 8 tablespoons of Ghee or use butter
- 1½ cups of almond flour 150g
- 1 cup of pecans 120g, chopped
- ½ cup of swerve Confectioners sweetener 78g
- 1 teaspoon of vanilla extract
- ½ teaspoon of vanilla liquid stevia
- ¼ teaspoon of salt
- Extra confectioners to roll balls in

Cooking Instructions:

1. Heat your oven to 350°F. Place all the recipe ingredients into food processor and process until batter forms a ball.

2. Pulse if needed. Taste batter and adjust sweetener if necessary. Line a baking sheet with parchment.

3. Use a cookie scoop and make 24 mounds. Roll each mound in the palm of your hand. Place in your freezer for about 20 to 30 minutes.

4. Place them in your oven for about 15 minutes or until golden around edges. When the time is up, allow to cool slightly.

5. Once able to handle roll each in some confectioner's sweetener. Allow to cool completely before storing in an air tight container.

6. Serve and enjoy!

Chocolate Chip

Preparation time: 5 minutes

Cooking time: 15 minutes

Total time: 20 minutes

Recipe Ingredients:

- ¼ cup of coconut flour
- ⅓ cup of unsalted butter, room temp.
- 3 tablespoon of Swerve sweetener
- 2 large eggs
- 3 tablespoon of sugar free chocolate chips
- ½ teaspoon of organic blackstrap molasses
- ¼ teaspoon of vanilla extract
- ⅛ teaspoon of salt

Cooking Instructions:

1. Heat your oven to 350°F. In a mixing bowl, mix together the dry ingredients of coconut flour, Swerve sweetener, chocolate chips, and salt.

2. Mix together the wet ingredients of unsalted butter, eggs, molasses, molasses, and vanilla extract in a medium bowl.

3. Slowly mix the wet ingredients into the dry ingredients. Using a cookie mat, place the cookies on while measuring two tbsp. of batter.

4. Bake in your oven for about 12 to 15 minutes or until browned on the bottom.

5. Serve and enjoy!

Flourless Chocolate Cookies

Preparation time: 10 minutes

Cooking time: 12 minutes

Total time: 22 minutes

Serves: 24

Recipe Ingredients:

- 1½ cups of powdered Swerve sugar substitute
- 6 tbsp. of unsweetened cocoa powder
- ¼ tsp. of salt
- ½ cup of very dark chocolate chips 63%
- ½ cup of chopped pecans
- 3 to 4 large egg whites
- 1 tsp. of vanilla extract

Cooking Instructions:

1. Heat your oven to 350°F. Cover baking sheet in baking parchment and spray with cooking spray.

2. In a medium bowl, mix the dry recipe ingredients, Swerve, cocoa, salt, chocolate chips, and pecans.

3. Add vanilla with three egg whites and stir to moisten batter. If it is as very thick or all the dry ingredients aren't moistened add one more egg white.

4. Place rounded tsp. of dough onto cookie sheet, 2"-3" apart as cookies will spread and thin while baking.

5. Bake for about 11 to 12 minutes. Cookies will still be soft in the center when removed from the oven.

6. When the time is up, allow them to set-up on the pan for about 5 to 8 minutes before removing to cooling rack

7. Serve and enjoy!

Almond Flour

Preparation time: 10 minutes

Cooking time: 12 minutes

Total time: 22 minutes

Serves: 18

Recipe Ingredients:

- 2½ cups of blanched almond flour
- 6 tablespoons of butter, softened
- ½ cup of Erythritol or other granular sweetener of choice
- 1 teaspoon of vanilla extract

Cooking Instructions:

1. Heat your oven to 350°F. Line a cookie sheet with parchment paper. Use a hand mixer to beat the butter and erythritol, until it's fluffy and light in color.

2. Beat in the vanilla extract. Beat in the almond flour, ½ cup (64g) at a time. (The dough will be dense and a little crumbly, but should stick when pressed together.)

3. Scoop rounded tablespoonful's of the dough onto the prepared cookie sheet. Flatten each cookie to about 1/3 in (.8 cm) thick.

4. Keep in mind they will not spread or thin out during baking, so make them as thin as you want them when done.

5. Bake for about 12 minutes, until the edges are golden. When the time is up, allow to cool completely in the pan before handling.

6. Serve and enjoy!

Peanut Butter Bacon Cookies

Preparation time: 10 minutes

Cooking time: 10 minutes

Overall time: 20 minutes

Yield: 12 Cookies

Recipe Ingredients:

- 6 slices of bacon, cooked crisp and crumbled
- 1 cup of chunky peanut butter (reduced sugar, natural)
- 1 cup of granular Swerve sweetener
- 1 large egg
- ½ cup of unsweetened organic cocoa powder
- 1½ teaspoon of vanilla extract
- 1 teaspoon of baking soda

Cooking Instructions:

1. Start by cooking bacon until crispy, crumble and set aside. Preheat oven to 350°F.

2. Then combine peanut butter, sweetener and egg in a mixing bowl. Mix until all ingredients are combined.

3. The peanut butter was thick and it just made it easier. To the mixture, add cocoa powder, vanilla extract and baking soda.

4. Mix until all ingredients are well combined. Mix in bacon crumbles. Line a baking sheet with a Silpat or parchment paper.

5. Form dough into 12 equal sized balls, place on liner and flatten just a bit. Bake for about 10 minutes.

6. When the time is up, remove from oven and place baking sheet on a cooling rack.

7. Allow the cookies to cool completely, serve and enjoy!

Bacon Onion Cookies

Preparation time: 15 minutes

Cooking time: 12 minutes

Total time: 27 minutes

Yield: 12 cookies

Recipe Ingredients:

- 1½ cup of almond flour (150g/5.3 oz)
- 1/3 cup of flaxmeal (50g/1.3 oz)
- 1 tablespoon of psyllium husk powder
- 1 tablespoon of onion powder
- 1 large eggs, free-range or organic
- 4 slices crisped up, crumbled bacon – bacon fat removed (32 g/1.1 oz)
- ½ teaspoon of sea salt or pink Himalayan rock salt
- Freshly ground pepper

Cooking Instructions:

1. Preheat your oven to 375°F. Line a baking tray with parchment paper. Lay the bacon slices on top of it and place in the oven.

2. Cook the bacon slices for about 10 to 15 minutes until crispy brown. When done, remove from the oven and set aside.

3. Reduce the temperature to 350°F. Place all the dry recipe ingredients into a bowl, almond flour, flax meal, psyllium husk powder, onion powder, salt and pepper.

4. Mix them together until well combined. If you don't have onion powder, you can use dried onion flakes and blend them until powdered.

5. Ensure not to use the whole psyllium husks – blend the psyllium husks until powdered if needed.

6. Add the egg and process well using your hands. Crumble or slice the bacon and add to the dough.

7. Process well using your hands. Reserve the bacon fat and use for other recipes. Using your hand, create 12 equal balls.

8. Place them on a baking sheet lined with parchment paper or silicone cookie sheet. Use a fork to press and flatten the dough.

9. Bake for about 10 to 12 minutes. Keep an eye on the cookies. Almond flour gets burnt easily and the cookies would taste bitter.

10. When done, the cookies should be golden brown. Store at room temp. in a container.

11. Serve and enjoy!

Butter Cookie Energy Bites

Preparation time: 10 minutes

Total time: 10 minutes

Serves: 8 Energy Bites

Recipe Ingredients:

- 1 cup of almond flour (We used Bob's Red Mill)
- 3 tablespoons melted butter
- 2 tablespoons of swerve sweetener
- 1 teaspoon vanilla extract
- Pinch of salt

Cooking Instructions:

1. In a small mixing bowl, combine all the recipe ingredients. The mixture should be wet enough to stick together.

2. Scoop out 1 tablespoon of the mixture at a time a roll into a ball. The balls should be 1¼ inch in diameter.

3. Refrigerate for 1 hour, if desired. Serve and enjoy!

Snickerdoodle Cookies

Preparation time: 10 minutes

Cooking time: 12 minutes

Total time: 22 minutes

Yield: 16 large cookies

Recipe Ingredients:

For the cookies:

- 2 medium eggs
- 2 teaspoons of vanilla extract
- 1 cup of almond butter
- ½ cup of almond milk
- ¼ cup of coconut oil, solid, at room temp.
- 1½ cup of golden monk fruit sweetener
- 1¾ cup of almond flour
- 1 cup of coconut flour
- 1 teaspoon of baking soda
- 2 teaspoons cream of tartar
- 1/8 teaspoon of pink Himalayan salt
- 1 teaspoon of cinnamon

For the coating:

- 3 tablespoons of golden monk fruit sweetener
- 1 tablespoon of cinnamon

Cooking Instructions:

1. Preheat your oven to 350°F. Line baking sheet with parchment paper.

2. In a medium mixing bowl, combine eggs, vanilla extract, almond butter, almond milk, and coconut oil. Mix them together with an electric mixer.

3. In a medium mixing bowl, whisk together the dry ingredients. In small batches, add dry ingredients to wet ingredients.

4. Use your hands to combine them together until dry ingredients are fully incorporated.

5. Place batter bowl in refrigerator to chill for about 15 minutes. Once chilled, form batter into medium-sized balls.

6. Roll ball in cinnamon sugar-coating mixture, and place on baking sheet. Once all balls are formed.

7. Use the palm of your hand or the bottom of a glass, flatten balls into cookies. Bake cookies for about 10 to 12 minutes.

8. When the time is up, remove from oven and allow to cool slightly before serving.

9. Serve and enjoy!

Chewy Pecan Cookies

Preparation time: 5 minutes

Cooking time: 12 minutes

Total time: 17 minutes

Yield: 20 cookies

Recipe Ingredients:

- 2 cups of (250g) ground pecans
- 1 large egg
- 1 tablespoon of salted butter, room temp.
- ½ teaspoon of baking soda
- ¼ cup of granulated sweetener (We used Sukrin gold)
- Optional: 20 additional pecan halves to decorate

Cooking Instructions:

1. Preheat your oven to 350°F. Grind pecan halves in the food processor.

2. We used scales to weigh them, but if you don't have scales, roughly 2½ cups of pecan.

3. Add all other ingredients and mix until well-combined. Form little balls in your hand and flatten into a cookie.

4. Place cookies onto a tray lined with baking/parchment paper. If desired, place a pecan half on each cookie.

5. Bake for about 9 to 12 minutes until slightly browned on the edges. The cookies are very soft when straight out of the oven.

6. Allow to cool completely before serving.

Pumpkin Cream Cheese

Preparation time: 10 minutes

Serves: 16 people

Recipe Ingredients:

- ½ cup of (56g) coconut flour
- 3 ounces (84g) cream cheese softened
- ½ cup of (112g) pumpkin puree
- ½ cup of (113g) butter, unsalted softened
- ½ cup of (107g) Xylitol/Erythritol
- 1 tsp. of vanilla extract
- 1½ tsp. of pumpkin spice
- ¼ tsp. of salt

Cooking Instructions:

1. Preheat your oven to 350°F. Line a baking tray with parchment paper.

2. In a medium mixing bowl, whisk the butter and erythritol. Add the cream cheese, vanilla extra and pumpkin and whisk until smooth.

3. Add the coconut flour, pumpkin spices and salt and beat until well combined. The mixture will be sticky. Wet your hands and take a ball of the dough.

4. Place on the baking tray and repeat for the remaining dough. Gently press down on the dough balls with a spoon. Use a fork to make a pattern.

5. Serve and enjoy!

BARS

Peanut Butter Chocolate Bars

Serves: 8

Recipe Ingredients:

For the Bars:

- ¾ cup of almond flour
- 2 ounces of butter
- ¼ cup of Swerve icing sugar style
- ½ cup of creamy peanut butter
- Vanilla extract

For the Topping:

- ½ cup of sugar-free chocolate chips

Cooking Instructions:

1. In a medium bowl, mix all the recipe ingredients for the bars together.

2. Spread into a small 6-inch pan, melt the chocolate chips in a microwave oven for 30 seconds and stir.

3. Add another 10 seconds if needed to melt fully. Spread the topping on top of the bars.

4. Refrigerate for at least an hour or two until the bars thicken up. Serve and enjoy!

S'mores Bars

Preparation time: 20 minutes

Cooking time: 45 minutes

Chill time: 2 hours

Total time: 3 hr. 40 minutes

Serves: 16

Recipe Ingredients:

Crust:

- 1½ cups of almond flour (We use Bob's Red Mill Super Fine)
- ¼ cup of granulated swerve sweetener
- ½ teaspoon of cinnamon
- ½ teaspoon of vanilla extract
- ¼ teaspoon of salt
- 5 tablespoons of butter chilled and cut into small pieces

Filling:

- ¾ cup of whipping cream
- 4 oz. of sugar-free dark chocolate (such as Lily's), chopped

Topping:

- 3 large egg whites at room temp.
- ¼ teaspoon of cream of tartar
- Pinch salt
- 3 tablespoons of granulated swerve sweetener
- 3 tablespoons of powdered swerve sweetener
- ½ teaspoon of vanilla extract

Cooking Instructions:

1. Crust: Preheat your oven to 325°F. Line a 9x9 square baking pan with parchment, leaving an overhang for easy removal.

2. Combine almond flour, sweetener, cinnamon, vanilla extract, and salt in a food processor. Pulse to combine.

3. Sprinkle with butter pieces and pulse until mixture resembles coarse crumbs. You can cut in butter with a pastry cutter.

4. Press into bottom of prepared baking pan. Bake for about 12 to 15 minutes, until the edges start to brown. Remove and allow it to cool while preparing topping.

5. Filling: In a small saucepan, bring cream to just a simmer. Add chopped chocolate and let sit 5 minutes to melt.

6. Whisk in until smooth. Spread over cooled crust and refrigerate until firm, for 1 hour.

7. Topping: Preheat your oven to 300°F. In a mixing bowl, beat egg whites with cream of tartar and salt until frothy. With beaters going, slowly.

8. Add sweeteners and vanilla extract and continue to beat until stiff peaks form. Spread over cooled filling.

9. Bake for about 20 minutes or until topping is golden. Refrigerate at least another hour to firm up.

10. Gently lift out by parchment paper edges and cut into squares.

11. Serve and enjoy!

Chocolate Fudge Protein Bars

Preparation time: 10 minutes

Total time: 10 minutes

Serves: 16

Recipe Ingredients:

- 4 oz. 114g raw unsalted sunflower seeds
- 4 oz. sun butter or tahini
- 2 scoops 2.7 oz. (75g) chocolate protein powder (We used Quest)
- 3 oz. unsweetened cocoa powder
- ¾ cup 3 oz. (80g) Sukrin Melis (powdered sugar free sweetener)
- ½ teaspoon of salt
- 8 tablespoons of 5.7 oz. (162g) softened coconut oil
- Optional Coating: ½ cup of sugar free chocolate chips and 1 tablespoon of butter

Cooking Instructions:

1. In your food processor, add all recipe ingredients and blend until smooth. Scrape down sides and blend again.

2. Taste and adjust sweetener if necessary. Pour batter into a parchment lined loaf pan. Refrigerate for about 30 minutes.

3. Slice into 8 bars then cut bars in half to make 16 bars. Freeze for about 30 minutes if you are planning on making optional coating.

4. If using optional coating, melt chocolate chips and butter in microwave for 1 minute. Stir until smooth and no lumps.

5. Dip the bottom half of the bars into the melted chocolate and lay on a parchment lined baking sheet. Drizzle more chocolate on top of bars if desired.

6. Serve and enjoy!

Cookie Bars

Preparation time: 10 minutes

Cooking time: 15 minutes

Total time: 25 minutes

Serves: 16 people

Recipe Ingredients

- ¾ cup of coconut butter
- ¼ cup of unsweetened apple sauce
- ¼ tsp. of grey sea salt
- 1¼ cup of raw sesame seeds

Optional:

- ½ tsp. of ground cinnamon
- ½ tsp. of vanilla extract
- 5 to 10 drops of alcohol-free stevia

Cooking Instructions:

1. Preheat your oven to 350°F. Set aside a 16-count silicon baking mold sheet. (You could use small muffin silicon molds if you desire).

2. In a large mixing bowl, add coconut butter, applesauce and sea salt. Add the optional ingredients if you desire.

3. Give everything a good stir until completely combined. Drop in sesame seeds and stir to coat. Press mixture into prepared sheet.

4. Bake in your oven for 10 to 15 minutes, until tops brown. Remove from the oven, keep in the molds.

5. Allow to cool for about 20 minutes. Then, transfer to the freezer for another 20 minutes to firm up.

6. Can be stored at room temperature. Serve and enjoy!

Twix Bars

Preparation time: 10 minutes

Cooking time: 35 minutes

Cooling time 1 hour

Total time: 45 minutes

Serves: 16 bars

Recipe Ingredients:

For the shortbread base:

- 2 cups/200g almond flour
- 1 medium egg
- 1 teaspoon of vanilla essence or vanilla bean powder

For the caramel:

- 1 cup 240ml coconut milk (full fat, from a can)
- 4 tablespoons of Sukrin fibre syrup
- Pinch of salt

For the chocolate topping:

- ¼ cup/60g coconut oil
- ¼ cup/20g cacao powder
- 1 tablespoon of Sukrin fibre syrup
- alternatively: 80g (1/3 cup melted chocolate, at least 85% cocoa solids

Cooking Instructions:

1. Preheat your oven to 350°F. First, make the shortbread base. Simply mix the almond flour with the egg and vanilla.

2. Roll out the dough between 2 sheets of baking paper or line a 9x6 inch pan with baking paper.

3. Press the dough down evenly. Bake for about 25 minutes or until lightly browned. For the caramel. Bring the coconut milk and fibre syrup to the boil.

4. Turn the heat down and let it bubble away gently until it has reduced by half. When the shortbread is done.

5. Remove it from the oven and let it cool down. Spread over the caramel and place in the fridge for about 10 minutes until it has firmed up.

6. For the chocolate topping. Heat coconut oil in a pan until liquid and add the cacao powder plus 1 tbsp. of fibre syrup.

7. Pour the melted chocolate over the caramel layer and let it firm up in the fridge. Cut into bars.

8. Serve and enjoy!

Magic Bars

Preparation time: 10 minutes

Cooking time: 33 minutes

Overall time: 43 minutes

Yield: 12 to 16 bars

Recipe Ingredients:

- 1½ cups of almond flour
- 2 tablespoons of sweetener of choice, or stevia equivalent
- 3 tablespoons of melted coconut oil
- ¼ teaspoon of salt
- ¾ cup of mini chocolate chips or sugar free chocolate chips
- ¼ cup of finely chopped walnuts, optional
- 2/3 cup full-fat shredded coconut
- 1¼ cup full-fat canned coconut milk
- 2 tablespoons of cocoa powder, optional

Cooking Instructions:

1. Line an 8-inch pan with parchment paper. Preheat oven to 350°F. Toss the almond flour, oil, salt, and sweetener in a mixing bowl. Press into the pan.

2. Sprinkle the chocolate chips, coconut, and optional nuts over top. Stir the coconut milk and cocoa together.

3. Pour the mixture evenly over top. Bake for about 33 minutes. When the time is up, remove from the oven and let sit 15 minutes to firm up.

4. Slice into bars, wiping the knife after each cut. Serve and enjoy!

Crunch Bars

Preparation time: 5 minutes

Cooking time: 5 minutes

Total time: 10 minutes

Serves: 20

Recipe Ingredients:

- 1½ cups of chocolate chips of choice
- 1 cup of almond butter, can sub for any nut or seed butter of choice
- ½ cup of sticky sweetener of choice
- ¼ cup of coconut oil
- 3 cups of nuts and seeds of choice almonds, cashews, pepitas

Cooking Instructions:

1. Line an 8 x 8-inch baking dish with parchment paper and set aside.

2. In a microwave-safe bowl, combine the chocolate chips of choice, almond butter, sticky sweetener and coconut oil.

3. Melt them until well combined. Add your nuts/seeds of choice and mix until fully combined.

4. Pour the keto crunch bar mixture into the lined baking dish and spread out using a spatula. Refrigerate or freeze until firm.

5. Serve and enjoy!

TARTS

Keto Tarts

Preparation time: 15 minutes

Cooking time: 15 minutes

Total time: 45 minutes

Recipe Ingredients:

For the keto tart crust:

- 2¼ cups of almond flour
- ¼ cup of powdered erythritol, (We used Swerve confectioners)
- 5 tablespoons of melted butter
- ¼ teaspoon of sea salt

For the Mascarpone cream:

- 6 ounces mascarpone cheese
- 2 tablespoons of powdered erythritol
- 1/3 cup of heavy cream
- 1 teaspoon of vanilla extract
- ¼ teaspoon of lemon zest, fresh

For garnishing:

- 3 strawberries, cut in half
- 6 blueberries
- 6 raspberries
- 6 blackberries

Cooking Instructions:

1. For the keto tart crust: Preheat your oven to 350°F. Spray six 4-inch tart pans with butter spray.

2. Combine the almond flour, butter, salt and sweetener together in a mixing bowl. Mix to incorporate.

3. Divide the dough between six tart pans and press down the bottom and walls. Make holes on the bottom of the dough, using a fork.

4. Bake for about 8 to 10 minutes, until golden, when the time is up. Remove from the oven and allow cool completely.

5. For the Mascarpone cream, beat mascarpone and powdered sweetener with an electric mixer for about 2 minutes on low speed.

6. Slowly add the heavy cream, beating on low speed. Increase the speed and beat for about 30 to 60 seconds, until the mixture is thick.

7. Be very careful, as at this point you may over beat the cream. Beat in the lemon zest and vanilla extract.

8. To assemble: Pipe mascarpone cream to fill the tartlets. Top with berries.

9. Serve and enjoy!

Lemon Curd Tarts

Preparation time: 10 minutes

Cooking time: 10 minutes

Total time: 20 minutes

Serves: 8 servings

Recipe Ingredients:

Crust:

- 1.5 cups blanched almond flour
- ¼ cup of Swerve confectioners
- ½ teaspoon of salt
- ¼ cup of unsalted butter melted
- 1 large egg

Filling:

- 4 tablespoons of salted butter
- 3 large eggs
- ½ cup of Swerve confectioners
- ¼ cup of lemon juice
- 1 tablespoon of lemon zest

Topping:

- 12 raspberries

Cooking Instructions:

1. Preheat your oven to 350°F. In a medium bowl, combine all of the crust ingredients, press into 4 (4 inch) mini tart pans.

2. Transfer to the oven, Bake for about 10 to 15 minutes until golden. When the time is up. Remove and let cool. Place the butter in a medium pot over low heat.

3. Once melted remove from the heat. Whisk in the Swerve confectioners, lemon juice, and lemon zest. Whisk in eggs and return to low heat.

4. Cook, stirring, until it thickens. Remove from heat and divide between the tarts. Refrigerate for one hour and top with raspberries. Serve and enjoy!

Cheesecake Tarts

Preparation time: 30 minutes

Cooking time: 30 minutes

Total time: 1 hour

Recipe Ingredients:

Crust:

- 3 tablespoons of butter, melted
- ¾ cup of almond flour

Filling:

- 12 ounces cream cheese, room temperature
- 1 medium egg
- ¼ cup of erythritol
- 1 teaspoon of vanilla extract
- 1 tablespoon of fresh lemon juice
- ¼ teaspoon of salt

Toppings:

- ¼ cup of sugar-free strawberry jam
- ¼ cup of blueberries

Cooking Instructions:

1. Preheat your oven to 350°F. Combine melted butter with almond flour, mix until it's crumbly, but combined.

2. Line a muffin tin with paper and press about 1 to 2 teaspoons of your almond flour crust mixture into each liner.

3. Bake in the oven for about 5 to 8 minutes or until golden brown. To make the cheesecake filling, beat 12 oz. of cream cheese with an electric hand mixer until soft.

4. Add in 1 egg. Mix together to combine well. Add ¼ cup of erythritol, or your favorite low carb sweetener, and mix.

5. Add 1 teaspoon of vanilla extract, 1 tablespoon of fresh lemon juice and ¼ teaspoon of salt and mix one last time.

6. Spoon your cheesecake filling onto the baked crusts. Bake for about 20 minutes. The cheesecakes will have risen and be set.

7. When the time is up, allow it to cool for about 10 minutes. Top each one with a teaspoon of sugar-free jam. We used strawberry.

8. Add some fresh fruit over that. We used 3 blueberries for each mini cheesecake. Let them chill in the fridge overnight.

9. Serve and enjoy!

Chocolate Tart

Preparation time: 6 minutes

Cooking time: 14 minutes

Total time: 20 minutes

Serves: 10 people

Recipe Ingredients:

Pie Crust Ingredients:

- 1 1/3 cups of almond flour
- 1½ teaspoon of coconut flour
- 3 tablespoons of cold butter
- 1.5 teaspoons of cold water

Ganache Ingredients:

- 4 ounces of sugar-free chocolate chips
- 4 ounces of heavy cream
- 1/3 cup of Trim Healthy Mama Gentle Sweet, finely ground

Cooking Instructions:

1. In your food processor, mix the ingredients until the dough comes together. The dough will go from crumbly to a ball.

2. Roll out or press into a pie plate. Bake the crust for about 12 to 14 minutes at 350°F until golden brown. When the time is up, allow to cool completely.

3. Heat the cream in the microwave for 2 minutes. Remove from heat and add the chocolate. Give everything a good stir until melted.

4. Add the sweetener and whisk until smooth and shiny. Pour over the cooled pie crust and spread evenly.

5. Chill for at least 30 minutes or until the chocolate has set. Top with fresh berries or whipped cream.

6. Serve and enjoy!

Tart Dough

Preparation time: 10 minutes

Cooking time: 1 min

Ready In: 11 min

Yields: 6

Recipe Ingredients:

- 1 cup of almond flour
- ⅛ teaspoon of salt
- ¼ teaspoon baking powder
- Butter, Salted 3 tablespoons
- I large raw egg
- ⅛ cup almond milk

Cooking Instructions:

1. In a stand mixer with a paddle attachment, combine the almond flour, salt, and baking powder.

2. Cut the butter into about 12 cubes, and mix them into the four. Undermix the butter so you are left with chunks that are 1-2 inches long.

3. Mix in the egg yolk. Then, 1 TB at a time, mix in the almond milk until the dough just comes together. Excess milk will make this dough soggy.

4. Use your hands to press the dough into a flat disc and wrap it in plastic wrap. Cool the tart dough entirely in the refrigerator before using it.

5. To defrost tart dough, let it thaw in a refrigerator. Baking times for tart dough vary, depending on your recipe.

Peanut Butter Tarts

Preparation time: 10 minutes

Cooking time: 8 minutes

Total time: 18 minutes

Recipe Ingredients:

Crust:

- ¼ cup of flaxseeds (or flaxseed meal)
- 2 tablespoons of almond flour
- 1 tablespoon of Erythritol
- 1 large egg white

Top Layer:

- 1 medium Avocado (about 130 grams)
- 4 tablespoons of cocoa powder
- ¼ cup of Erythritol
- ½ teaspoon of vanilla extract
- ½ teaspoon of cinnamon
- 2 tablespoons of heavy cream

Middle Layer:

- 4 tablespoons of peanut butter
- 2 tablespoons of butter

Cooking Instructions:

1. Preheat the oven to 350°F. To make your crust, grind ¼ cup of flaxseeds until they become mealy.

2. Then, add the rest of the crust ingredients to the flaxseeds and mix thoroughly. Press crust mixture into tart pans and up the sides.

3. Bake in your oven for about 8 minutes or until set. While the crust is baking, combine all the top layer ingredients in a small blender, blend until smooth.

4. Once the crusts are out of the oven, allow the crust to cool. Then melt peanut butter and butter in the microwave until soft.

5. Pour the melted peanut butter layer onto your tart crusts and place in the fridge for 30 minutes until the top is set.

6. Once the top of the peanut butter layer is set, add the chocolate avocado layer on top and smooth out. Place in the fridge for another 30 minutes.

7. Serve and enjoy!

Hazelnut Tart

Preparation time: 10 minutes

Yield: 8 servings

Recipe Ingredients:

- 4 keto mini pie crusts
- 2 tbsp. of (30 ml) coconut oil, melted
- 2 tbsp. of (30 ml) coconut cream, melted
- 2 oz. (56 g) 100% chocolate, melted
- Erythritol, to taste
- ¼ cup of (60 ml) hazelnut butter

Cooking Instructions:

1. In a mixing bowl, mix the coconut oil, coconut cream, chocolate, and erythritol together.

2. Pour 1 tbsp. of hazelnut butter in each tart crust. Then pour the chocolate mixture on top of the hazelnut butter filling up the tart crust.

3. Refrigerate for 2 hours until solid. Serve and enjoy!

Tart Crust

Preparation time: 10 minutes

Cooking time: 15 minutes

Total time: 25 minutes

Serves: 12

Recipe Ingredients:

- 1 to ½ cups of almond flour
- ½ cup of coconut flour
- 5 tablespoons of erythritol, powdered
- 2 large eggs
- 4 tablespoons of unsalted butter, cold
- ½ teaspoon of vanilla extract

Cooking Instructions:

1. Preheat your oven to 350°F. Spray a 10-inch tart pan with removable bottom with cooking spray. Set aside.

2. Add in all the recipe ingredients to the bowl of a food processor. Pulse until dough comes together.

3. Using spoon, press into the bottom and up sides of greased tart pan. Bake crust in your oven at 350°F for about 15 minutes.

4. Bake until top and edges just begin to brown. Remove from oven and let cool for about 10 minutes.

5. Remove tart from pan and fill as desired.

Caramel Tarts

Preparation time: 8 minutes

Cooking time: 20 minutes

Serves: 24

Recipe Ingredients:

Chocolate Base:

- 100g of almond meal
- 20g sweetener of choice
- 25g of coconut desiccated
- 1 tbsp. of unsweetened cocoa
- 65g of butter melted

Caramel:

- 60g sweetener, I use Sukrin
- 200g of butter
- 200g thickened or heavy cream

Topping:

- 100g chocolate keto chocolate, dark chocolate or keto white chocolate

Cooking Instructions:

1. Preheat your oven to 170°C. In a large mixing bowl, mix all base ingredients together. Spoon 2 tsp. of mix into each hole in silicone tray.

2. Press firmly into mould. Bake for about 10 to 15 minutes or until golden. Reserve while making caramel.

3. Combine butter and sweetener in a saucepan over medium - high heat. Continue to whisk and watch the caramel until it starts to turn a slight amber color.

4. Whisk for about 5 minutes, whisk in cream and continue to whisk for about 4 to 6 minutes until caramel thickens and coats the back of a spoon.

5. Spoon 1 tbsp. of caramel onto each tart base. Transfer to fridge and refrigerate for 3 hours.

6. Melt chocolate and top each tart with a tsp. of chocolate. Refrigerate until set.

7. Serve and enjoy!

PIES

Strawberry Pie

Preparation time: 10 minutes

Cooking time: 20 minutes

Total time: 30 minutes

Serves: 12 slices

Recipe Ingredients:

- 1 recipe coconut flour pie crust, or any crust of your choice
- 2 pounds of strawberries, fresh or frozen
- 1 cup of powdered erythritol, or any sweetener of choice
- 3 tablespoons of vital proteins grass-fed gelatin
- ½ cup of water
- 2 tablespoons of lemon juice

Cooking Instructions:

1. In a large saucepan over medium heat, simmer the strawberries with powdered erythritol for about 15 minutes or until strawberries are soft.

2. Stir occasionally. While strawberries simmer, whisk the gelatin, water, and lemon juice together in a small mixing bowl.

3. Let sit for a couple minutes to thicken. Whisk the gelatin mixture into the strawberries. Simmer for a couple minutes,

4. Stir and whisk continuously until the gelatin dissolves. Let the strawberry filling and pie crust cool separately for about 20 minutes.

5. Pour the strawberry filling into the baked pie crust. Cool on the counter, then refrigerate overnight to set.

6. Garnish with whipped cream and fresh strawberries. Serve and enjoy!

Butter Pie

Preparation time: 15 minutes

Cooking time: 45 minutes

Additional time: 2 hours

Total time: 3 hours

Yield: 8 servings

Recipe Ingredients:

For the crust:

- 1¼ cup of almond flour
- ¼ cup of butter, melted
- 1 large egg
- 3 tablespoons of lakanto golden Monk fruit sweetener

For the filling:

- ½ cups of lakanto golden Monk fruit sweetener
- 12 tablespoons of butter, melted
- 8 ounces cream cheese, softened
- 1 large egg
- 1 egg yolk

Cooking Instructions:

1. Preheat your oven to 375°F. Then mix all of the crust ingredients together in medium bowl.

2. Use the mixture to create a crust in the bottom of a 9" glass pie plate. Bake the crust in your oven for about 7 minutes.

3. When the time is up, remove crust from oven and reduce temp to 350°F. In a separate bowl, use a hand mixer to combine all of the filling ingredients.

4. Mix well to combine, pour into the pie plate over the crust. Place back into your oven for about 35 to 40 minutes.

5. Bake until the top starts to turn golden to golden brown. Remove from oven and let cool for at least 1 to 2 hours. Slice and enjoy!

Spinach Pie

Preparation time: 15 minutes

Cooking time: 35 minutes

Total time: 50 minutes

Yield: 16 servings

Recipe Ingredients:

Crust:

- 2½ cup of blanched almond flour
- ½ teaspoon of sea salt
- ¼ cup of coconut oil, melted
- 1 large egg, beaten

Filling:

- 1 pound of frozen spinach, defrosted and squeezed to remove water
- 8 ounces feta cheese, crumbled
- 4 ounces cream cheese, cut into very small cubes
- 2 ounces mozzarella cheese, shredded
- 4 cloves of garlic, minced
- 1 tablespoon of fresh dill, chopped
- 4 large egg, beaten

Cooking Instructions:

1. Preheat your oven to 350°F. Line the bottom of a 9 in (23 cm) round pie pan or 8 in (20 cm) square pan with parchment paper.

2. Mix together the almond flour and sea salt in a large mixing bowl. Stir in the melted coconut oil and egg, until well combined.

3. Mix them together until it's uniform. Press the dough into the bottom of the prepared pan.

4. Bake for about 10 to 12 minutes, until lightly golden. Meanwhile, stir together all the filling ingredients, adding the eggs last.

5. Transfer the filling into it and smooth the top. Then bake for about 30 to 40 minutes, until the center is firm. When the time is up, serve and enjoy!

Coconut Custard Pie

Preparation time: 10 minutes

Cooking time: 45 minutes

Total time: 55 minutes

Serves: 8 people

Recipe Ingredients:

- 2 large eggs
- 1 cup of coconut milk canned
- ¾ cup of low carb sugar substitute
- ¼ cup of coconut flour
- 2 tbsp. of unsalted butter melted and cooled
- 1 tsp. of vanilla extract
- ¾ tsp. of baking powder
- 1 tsp. of lemon zest
- ½ tsp. of lemon extract
- 4 oz. of unsweetened shredded coconut

Cooking Instructions:

1. Spray a 9-inch pie dish with cooking spray and preheat your oven to 350°F.

2. In a mixing bowl, mix together the eggs, coconut milk, sweetener, coconut flour, butter, baking powder, vanilla, lemon zest, and lemon extract.

3. Stir just until combined. Fold in the unsweetened coconut. Pour the mixture into the pie dish.

4. Bake for about 40 to 45 minutes or until the edges are brown and the top is a light golden brown.

5. When the time is up, remove from the oven and allow to cool completely before cutting.

6. Serve and enjoy.

Almond Butter Pie

Preparation time: 10 minutes

Cooking time: 30 minutes

Total time: 40 minutes

Yield: 12 slices

Recipe Ingredients:

For the Crust:

- ¾ cup (75g) coconut flour
- 2 tablespoons (10g) psyllium husk
- ½ cup of coconut oil
- ½ cup of water
- Pinch of salt

For the Filling:

- 2 oz. (30g) unsweetened chocolate (We use the Ghiradelli 100%)
- 1 can (400ml) full fat coconut milk
- ¼ cup of coconut oil
- 1 cup of almond butter
- ¼ teaspoon of stevia (optional)

Cooking Instructions:

1. Preheat your oven to 350°F. Melt together water and coconut oil in a mixing bowl. Stir in psyllium husk until a sort of gel forms.

2. Stir in coconut flour and salt and let sit for about 1 to 2 minutes until all the liquid has been absorbed. Press the crust into a 9" pie dish.

3. Try to make the crust as uniformly thick as possible so that it bakes evenly. Poke the bottom of the crust a bunch of times with a fork. Bake for about 30 minutes.

4. While the crust is baking, combine remaining ingredients in a high-speed blender and process until they are thoroughly combined.

5. Remove the crust from the oven and let cool for a few minutes before pouring in the filling. Chill in the fridge for about 6 to 8 hours until set for 3 hours.

Almond Flour Pie Crust

Preparation time: 5 minutes

Cooking time: 10 minutes

Total time: 15 minutes

Serves: 12 slices

Recipe Ingredients:

- 2½ cup of blanched almond flour
- 1/3 cup of erythritol, or any sweetener of choice
- ¼ teaspoon of sea salt or ½ teaspoon for savory pie crust
- ¼ cup of ghee measured solid, then melted
- 1 large egg (or ~2 tablespoons of additional ghee)
- ½ teaspoon of vanilla extract (optional)

Cooking Instructions:

1. Preheat your oven to 350°F. Line the bottom of a 9 in (23 cm) round pie pan with parchment paper.

2. Mix together the almond flour, erythritol (if using), and sea salt in a large mixing bowl. Stir in the melted ghee and egg, until well combined.

3. If using vanilla, stir that into the melted ghee before adding to the dry ingredients. The "dough" will be dry and crumbly.

4. Continue mixing, pressing and stirring, until it's uniform and there is no almond flour powder left.

5. Press the dough into the bottom of the prepared pan. You can flute the edges if desired, if it crumbles when doing this, just press it back together.

6. Carefully poke holes in the surface using a fork to prevent bubbling. Bake for about 10 to 12 minutes, until lightly golden.

7. Add fillings only after pre-baking. Serve and enjoy!

Chocolate Pie Crust

Preparation time: 5 minutes

Cooking time 12 minutes

Total time: 17 minutes

Recipe Ingredients:

- 2 cups of sunflower seed flour or use almond if no nut allergies
- 1/8 tsp. of salt
- 2 tbsp. of butter unsalted, softened
- 1 medium egg
- ¼ cup of unsweetened cocoa powder
- ½ cup of swerve or erythritol or ½ tsp. of pure stevia extract

Cooking Instructions:

1. Preheat your oven to 350°F. Add all recipe ingredients into a food processor and process until smooth.

2. Grease a 9-inch pie pan and press mixture into pan as evenly as possible. Use a fork and make holes into the bottom.

3. Bake for about 10 to 12 minutes. When the time is up, allow to cool completely before adding filling.

4. Serve and enjoy!

FROZEN DESSERTS

Vanilla Ice Cream

Preparation time: 30 minutes

Cooking time: 15 minutes

Chill time: 5 hours

Total time: 45 minutes

Serves: 6 to 8 servings

Recipe Ingredients:

- 1 recipe sugar-free condensed milk
- 1½ cups of heavy cream
- 3 tablespoons of powdered swerve sweetener
- 1½ tablespoons of vodka (optional, helps reduce iciness)
- ½ teaspoon of vanilla extract
- 1/8 teaspoon of salt

Cooking Instructions:

1. Make the sweetened condensed milk according to the directions and let cool to room temp.

2. Whisk in the heavy cream, powdered sweetener, vodka, vanilla extract, and salt. Taste and adjust sweetener if needed.

3. You can use additional Bocha Sweet or allulose here but because it's granular, you will need to whisk for a while to dissolve it properly.

4. Chill the mixture at least one hour and up to overnight, then pour into the canister of an ice cream maker.

5. Churn according to manufacturer's directions. If you have the kind of ice cream maker that requires the canister to be frozen first, don't forget to do that!

6. Transfer to an airtight container and freeze until firm, at least 4 hours.

7. Serve and enjoy!

Butter Pecan Ice Cream

Serves: 8 people

Recipe Ingredients:

- ¼ cup of butter
- 2 cups of heavy cream
- ½ cup of swerve sweetener confectioners
- ¼ teaspoon of salt
- 2 egg yolks
- 2 teaspoons of maple extract
- 1 tablespoon of choczero maple pecan sweetener or sweetener of choice
- 1 tablespoon of MCT oil
- 2 tablespoons of pecans toasted, chopped

Cooking Instructions:

1. In a small sauce pan, melt the butter, heavy cream, Swerve sweetener and salt. Heat over low heat and do not boil.

2. Whisk egg yolks until light in color. Take a spoonful of the butter cream mixture. Stir in spoonful of butter into the yolks to temper them.

3. Continue with a few more spoonsful. Gradually add in the remaining yolk into the mixture on the stove.

4. Continue to stir until mixture thickens over low heat, and coats the back of a spoon, 175°F. Pour into a bowl to cool in the fridge for about 30 minutes.

5. Then add maple extract and Choczero sweetener or sweetener of choice and MCT oil. Once combined, pour the mixture into your ice cream machine.

6. Follow manufacturer's instructions. Stir in pecans then spread ice cream into an 8 by 5 loaf pan and freeze for about 2 to 3 hours.

7. Serve and enjoy!

Chocolate Mason Jar Ice Cream

Preparation time: 8 minutes

Total time: 8 minutes

Yield: 2 cups

Recipe Ingredients:

- 1 cup of heavy cream
- 2 tbsp. of granular erythritol
- 1 tbsp. of unsweetened cocoa powder
- 1 tsp. of pure vanilla extract
- 2 tbsp. of sugar free chocolate chips, optional (We use this brand)

Cooking Instructions:

1. Combine all recipe ingredients in a wide mouth pint sized mason jar. Screw the lid on and shake vigorously for about 5 minutes.

2. The liquid in side should double in volume, filling the mason jar. Freeze for about 3 to 24 hours.

3. Scoop and enjoy!

Strawberry Ice Cream

Preparation time: 5 minutes

Freeze: 2 hours

Total time: 5 minutes

Serves: 3

Recipe Ingredients:

- 1 cup of heavy cream
- 1 cup of strawberries diced about 5 large
- 1 tsp. of vanilla
- 1 tsp. of liquid Stevia

Cooking Instructions:

1. Cut your strawberries into pieces and pour the heavy cream into mason jar.

2. Add strawberries to mason jar. Add vanilla to mason jar. Add Liquid Stevia to mason jar.

3. Secure the Lid on mason jar, shake vigorously for about 5 minutes. Leave top on mason jar and put in freezer for about 2 to 3 hours.

4. Serve and enjoy!

Lime Popsicles

Recipe Ingredients:

Makes: 6 popsicles

- 2 large ripe avocados (400g/14.2oz)
- zest from 1 lime, organic
- juice from 2 limes
- 440 ml coconut milk
- ½ cup of powdered Erythritol or swerve (80g/ 2.8oz)
- 15 to 20 drops liquid Stevia

Cooking Instructions:

1. Halve the avocados and remove the seeds. Scoop the soft pulp into a bowl. Add the coconut milk, fresh lime peel and juice, powdered Erythritol and stevia.

2. Using a hand blender, pulse until smooth. Using a spoon, fill in the popsicle molds. Insert a wooden stick into each of them.

3. Place them in the freezer for about 3 to 4 hours or until frozen. Serve and enjoy!

Raspberry Ripple Ice Cream

Yield: 10 bars

Preparation time: 20 minutes

Additional time: 4 hours

Total time: 4 hr. 20 minutes

Recipe Ingredients:

- 2 cups of heavy cream
- 4 cups of raspberries (2 cups of juice)
- ½ cup of erythritol
- 1 teaspoon of vanilla

Cooking Instructions:

1. Start by cooking raspberries over a low heat with a half cup of water. Cook the raspberries until the juices release.

2. Press the raspberries through a sieve, and press out the raspberries juice. Reserve 2 cups of raspberry juice.

3. Optional, add 1 tablespoon of vodka if you desire. Mix heavy whipping cream with vanilla and powdered erythritol and separate into 2 bowls.

4. Optional, add 1 tablespoon of vodka if you desire. Add ½ cup of raspberry juice to one of the bowls of cream, and 1½ cup to the other.

5. Pour mixtures into a popsicle mold alternating between the colors. Pour the mixtures gently.

6. Freeze until solid. Remove from popsicle mold and store wrapped with a bit of parchment in a freezer bag for up to a month.

7. Serve and enjoy!

Shamrock Shake

Preparation time: 5 minutes

Total time: 5 minutes

Yield: 1 shake

Recipe Ingredients:

- ½ medium avocado
- 1 scoop dairy free vanilla protein powder (about 30g)
- ½ cup of silk almond coconut milk
- 8 ice cubes
- 1/8 tsp. of peppermint extract
- 5 drops of natural green food coloring (optional for color)
- 2 tbsp. of coconut milk whipped cream (optional)
- 1 tbsp. of sugar-free dark chocolate chips

Cooking Instructions:

1. In your blender, combine the avocado, protein powder, almond coconut milk, ice, peppermint extract and food coloring.

2. Pulse until blended and creamy. Top with dairy free whipped cream and sugar-free chocolate chips, if using.

3. Serve and enjoy!

Ice Cream Sandwiches

Preparation time: 30 minutes

Total time: 30 minutes

Serves: 16 people

Recipe Ingredients:

Cookie Dough Ingredients:

- 4 tablespoons of butter
- 4 tablespoons of cream cheese
- 2 cups of almond flour
- ½ cup of trim healthy mama gentle sweet
- 1 teaspoon of molasses
- 1 teaspoon of vanilla
- 1 cup of sugar free chocolate chips or chopped sugar free or dark chocolate

Ice Cream Ingredients:

- 2 cups of heavy cream
- 1 cup half and half
- 1 cup of almond milk
- 3 egg yolks
- ½ cup trim healthy mama gentle sweet
- 1 tablespoon of vanilla
- 1 tablespoon of glycerin
- 1 cup of sugar free chocolate chips, optional

Cooking Instructions:

1. Line 8x8 square baking pan with parchment paper. Using an electric mixer, beat butter, cream cheese, and sweetener together.

2. Add in the almond flour, sweetener, vanilla, and molasses. Mix together to combine. Stir in the chocolate chips.

3. Put half the cookie dough in the bottom of the pan and spread gently. Cover with another layer of parchment.

4. Spread the rest of the dough onto the second layer. Put this in the freezer. Make the ice cream.

5. For the Ice Cream, combine all the ice cream ingredients in a blender. Blend until smooth.

6. Pour into an ice cream machine and churn according to the manufacturer's instructions. Add the additional chocolate chips during the last minute if desired.

7. When the ice cream has gotten firm remove the cookie dough from the freezer. Remove the top layer.

8. Then pour ¾ of the ice cream on top of the bottom layer of cookie dough. Reserve the rest in another container.

9. You need it to firm up a little more. So put this and the top layer of dough in the freezer separately.

10. After an hour or two remove them from the freezer and top the ice cream with the top layer of cookie dough. Freeze for an additional 3 to 4 hours.

11. This is when it's nice that there was a bit of ice cream left over. It's so hard to be that patient. Eat a little of the extra while you wait.

12. Remove from the freezer and cut into squares with a sharp knife. Wrap individually with plastic wrap to store.

13. Serve and enjoy!

CUSTARDS & MOUSSES

Vanilla Cheesecake Mousse

Preparation time: 15 minutes

Total time: 15 minutes

Serves: 6 servings

Recipe Ingredients:

Blueberry Sauce:

- 1 cup of fresh blueberries plus 10 more for garnish (2 per serving) if desired
- ½ tbsp. of erythritol
- ½ tsp. of pure vanilla extract
- ¼ tsp. of real fruit natural pectin
- 1 drop stevia glycerite

Vanilla Cheesecake Mousse:

- 8 oz. 227g full-fat organic grass-fed cream cheese
- 2 tbsp. of erythritol
- 1 tsp. of pure vanilla extract
- 3 drops of stevia glycerite
- 1 cup of 237 ml organic grass-fed heavy whipping cream

Cooking Instructions:

1. In your food processor, puree all ingredients for the blueberry sauce and set aside. The blueberry sauce will thicken slightly as it sits.

2. Unwrap the cream cheese, place it in a large bowl. Microwave on high for about 30 seconds to soften it. Add the erythritol, vanilla, and stevia glycerite.

3. Beat with a handheld electric mixer until smooth. Beat the heavy cream to stiff peaks in a separate medium bowl.

4. Beat ¼ of the whipped cream into the cream cheese mixture until smooth. Use a rubber spatula to fold in the remaining whipped cream ¼ at a time.

5. Transfer the mousse to 5 individual glasses. Divide the blueberry sauce on top. Garnish each with 2 blueberries if desired. Serve and enjoy!

Chocolate Custard

Preparation time: 5 minutes plus chilling time

Total time: 35 minutes

Makes: 4 servings

Recipe Ingredients:

- ½ cup of whole milk or unsweetened soy milk
- 3 large eggs
- 3½ oz. of dark chocolate (at least 70% cacao), broken into small pieces
- 1 medium peach, pitted and sliced, or about 1 cup other seasonal fruit,
- Garnish with fresh whipped cream

Cooking Instructions:

1. Heat the milk in a small saucepan over medium heat, stirring regularly, until tiny bubbles form on the side of the pan.

2. Remove from heat, whisk the eggs in a small mixing bowl and set aside. Melt the chocolate in a double boiler, then remove from the heat.

3. While whisking, slowly add the milk 3 tbsp. at a time to the melted chocolate, whisking until all the milk has been added.

4. While whisking continuously, slowly add the whisked eggs to the melted chocolate mixture. Place back over very low heat and cook.

5. Stir regularly, for about 5 minutes, or until the mixture thickens. Remove from the heat.

6. Pour the mixture into four small ramekins. Refrigerate for about 20 minutes or until fully cooled.

7. Garnish with peach slices before serving. Serve and enjoy!

Coconut Mousse

Preparation time: 15 minutes

Cooking time: 5 minutes

Cooling: 3 hours

Total time: 3 hours 20 minutes

Serves: 6 people

Recipe Ingredients:

- 1½ cups of coconut cream
- 1 tbsp. + 1 tsp. of gelatin powder
- ¼ cup of natvia
- 1 tsp. of vanilla essence
- 1 tsp. of coconut essence
- 1½ cups of heavy cream
- 1 tbsp. of unsweetened shredded coconut toasted
- 4 keto coconut wafers, optional
- ½ cup of keto whipped cream, optional

Cooking Instructions:

1. Place the coconut cream, gelatin, natvia, vanilla, and coconut essence in a small saucepan over medium heat. Bring to a simmer.

2. Ensure that the gelatin has dissolved, then remove from the heat. Allow it to cool at room temp.

3. Place the cream in a large mixing bowl, using a hand mixer, whisk to firm soft peaks. Add a little of the coconut mixture at a time and whisk through to combine.

4. Pour into 4 serving glasses or ramekins. Cover and set in the fridge for about 3 hours. Serve garnished with a keto coconut wafer and whipped cream.

5. Serve and enjoy!

Crème Anglaise Custard

Recipe Ingredients:

- 3 extra large egg yolks (65g)
- 300g double cream
- 2 tablespoons of (20g) Sukrin icing 'sugar'
- 1 vanilla pod or 1 teaspoon of vanilla paste
- Pinch of fine Himalayan pink salt

Cooking Instructions:

1. Using an electric whisk, whip up egg yolks with icing 'sugar' and salt until pale and foamy.

2. Place the cream and vanilla seeds in a small heavy-base saucepan. Heat the cream whilst stirring, until it starts to release steam,

3. But before it begins to simmer. Pour the hot cream into the whipped yolks whilst whisking by hand.

4. Transfer the crème anglaise back to the saucepan you used for the cream. Turn the heat on to medium.

5. Continue whisking while you let it simmer gently, remove from heat as soon as it thickens for about 60 seconds. When the time is up.

6. Serve over your favorite dessert and enjoy!

Peanut Butter Mousse

Preparation time: 5 minutes

Total time: 5 minutes

Serves: 4 servings

Recipe Ingredients:

- ½ cup of heavy whipping cream, more if necessary
- 4 oz. cream cheese, softened
- ¼ cup of natural peanut butter, no sugar added
- ¼ cup of powdered swerve sweetener
- ½ teaspoon of vanilla extract

Cooking Instructions:

1. In a mixing bowl, whip the ½ cup of cream until it holds stiff peaks. Set aside.

2. In a separate mixing bowl, beat together the cream cheese and peanut butter until smooth and creamy. Then add the sweetener and vanilla.

3. Add a pinch of salt if your peanut is unsalted. Beat until smooth. If your mixture is overly thick, add about 2 tablespoons of heavy cream to lighten it.

4. Beat until well combined. Gently fold in the whipped cream until no streaks remain. Spoon or pipe into little dessert glasses.

5. Drizzle with a little low carb chocolate sauce, if desired.

6. Serve and enjoy!

Pumpkin Cheesecake Mousse

Preparation time: 5 minutes

Total time: 5 minutes

Serves: 12 people

Recipe Ingredients:

- 16 oz. of cream cheese, room temperature
- 15 oz. of canned pumpkin not pumpkin pie filling
- 2 cups of heavy cream
- ¼ teaspoon of salt
- 2 tsp. of pumpkin pie spice or use cinnamon, ginger, nutmeg, cloves
- 1 to 2 tsp. of pumpkin spice liquid stevia or vanilla stevia to taste
- 1 tsp. of vanilla extract
- Optional toppings: Sukrin gold brown sugar substitute

Cooking Instructions:

1. In a stand mixer, blend cream cheese and pumpkin until smooth. Add the rest of the ingredients.

2. Blend until whipped and fluffy for about 5 minutes. Taste and adjust sweetener if needed.

3. Pipe into serving glasses and top with cacao nibs or brown sugar sub like Sukrin if desired.

4. Serve and enjoy!

Egg Custard

Preparation time: 5 minutes

Cooking time: 30 minutes

Total time: 35 minutes

Serves: 4 people

Recipe Ingredients:

- 4 medium eggs
- ½ cup of cream or half and half
- 2 cups of unsweetened almond milk
- ⅓ cup of Splenda or your favorite low-calorie sugar substitute
- 1 tsp. of vanilla extract
- ¼ tsp. of cinnamon

Cooking Instructions:

1. Preheat your oven to 350°F. Grease 4 custard cups and place in a 9 X 12 baking dish.

2. Pour enough water around the custard cups that it comes about ½ inch up the side of the cups.

3. Add all the ingredients in a large mixing bowl, whisk together well. Pour into custard cups.

4. Bake for about 30 minutes or until the eggs are set. Remove from oven when the time is up.

5. Allow to cool before serving. Serve and enjoy!

Mascarpone Mousse

Preparation time: 10

minutes Total time: 10

minutes Serves: 8 people

Recipe Ingredients:

For the chocolate mascarpone mousse:

- 250g/8.8 oz. mascarpone
- 250g /8.8 oz. double/heavy cream
- 4 tablespoons of unsweetened cocoa powder
- 4 tablespoons of powdered erythritol

For the vanilla mousse:

- 100g/3.5 oz. cream cheese
- 100g /3.5 oz. double/heavy cream
- 1 teaspoon of vanilla extract
- 2 tablespoons of powdered erythritol

Cooking Instructions:

1. In your electric mixer, add in all ingredients for the chocolate mascarpone mousse whisk until well combined and the whipping cream starts to thicken.

   Stop whisking when you have a creamy consistency. Do not over-mix! Whisk e whipping cream for the vanilla mousse.

   he cream cheese, vanilla extract and powdered sweetener last. Fill te mousse into serving glasses, dolloping the vanilla mousse on top.

   a knife until you have a marble effect. Serve and enjoy!

www.ingramcontent.com/pod-product-compliance
Lightning Source LLC
Chambersburg PA
CBHW081754100526
44592CB00015B/2428